Praying the Franciscan Crown Rosary

Victoria L. Spalding, O.F.S.

DEDICATION

In loving and joyful memory of all living and deceased
Franciscans, especially all past and present members of
Mt. St. Sepulchre Fraternity in Washington, D.C.

CONTENTS

ACKNOWLEDGMENTS

With grateful heart to Fr. Angelus Shaughnessy, OFM Cap, who has been a great support in my Franciscanism and love of God.

FOREWORD
Fr. Angelus Shaughnessy, O.F.M Cap

Mary, the Mother of God had her sorrows. She had also her joys. We would expect Her joys too because joy is the infallible sign of the Christian, and Mary was the perfect follower of Jesus. Mary knows that the Christian has only one duty; to be full of joy. St. Francis of Assisi knew that too; and that is why he said, "It is for the devil and his ilk to be sad but for us always to rejoice in the Lord." Mary and Francis knew that the ultimate victory belongs to Jesus Christ; and if we stay with Jesus, we too share his victory. He it was who overcame death, sin, Satan, and hell. The Seven Joys of the Franciscan Crown Rosary show what contribution Mary made to that victory. May She teach us to live this joy in our lives, too. The Lord reward Victoria Spalding for sharing her insights from our Heavenly Mother.

Victoria L. Spalding, OFS

Franciscan Crown Rosary

As a Franciscan, one of the ways we honor the joys of Our Lady is by praying the Franciscan Crown Rosary. The recitation of *The Franciscan Crown Rosary* dates to the early part of the 15th century. A young man, who use to find joy in weaving a crown of wild flowers for a beautiful statue of Mary, decided to enter the Franciscan order. Upon entering the community, however, he was saddened and upset because he was no longer able to find enough time to gather flowers for his personal devotion to Our Lady.

The young novice, while struggling with the idea of abandoning his vocation, suddenly experienced a vision of the Blessed Virgin Mary. She encouraged the young novice to persevere by reminding him of the joyfulness of the Franciscan spirit. She also instructed him to meditate daily on seven joyful events from her own life as a new form of the rosary. Instead of a crown of flowers, the novice would now weave a crown of prayers. Before long, many other Franciscans began to pray the *Crown* and soon it spread to the entire Order, becoming officially established in 1422.

The Franciscan Crown Rosary consists of seven joyful mysteries. Each decade is preceded by an Our Father and followed by a Glory Be. The Crown recalls the seven joys of Mary and how she responded to the grace of God in her life. At the end of the seven decades, there are two additional Hail Mary's, bringing the total of Hail Mary's to 72 years, to honor Our Lady's life on earth. The Crown concludes by praying one Our Father and one Hail Mary for the intentions of the Holy Father, the Pope.

The seven joyful mysteries are:

The Annunciation

The Visitation

The Nativity

The Visit of the Magi

The Finding of Jesus in the Temple

The Resurrection

The Assumption and the Coronation

The following are meditations on the seven joyful mysteries of the Franciscan Crown Rosary, each followed by an interior meditation from Our Lady taken while in prayer.

1st *Joyful Mystery - The Annunciation*

Mary was an only child, born of St. Joachim and St. Anne. She was consecrated to the temple when she was three years old, so that she might be among one of the holy virgins who would serve God. She spent her time there, doing manual labor and reading spiritual works. Later, we are told she was espoused to St. Joseph. Mary knew the Jewish religion well. She had been told of the promise for a long awaited Messiah, one who would free the Jews from the oppression of their enemies.

At the first sight of the angel, Mary experiences a sense of fear. The angel greets her, "Hail, favored one! The Lord is with you", indicating that Mary is "full of grace" and highly favored by God. This greeting would have been impossible if Mary had ever been tainted by sin, since every form of sin diminishes grace. The angel bows to her, a young virgin, a mere mortal human being. Mary considers that this could possibly be a deception of the evil one, and she ponders what kind of greeting this might be. Her humility does not allow her to even recognize her own importance in God's plan of salvation for His people.

The angel quickly removes Mary's fears, by engaging in conversation with her and by answering her questions. Unlike Eve, who conversed with the devil without considering the danger, Mary carefully judges whether this is from God or not before giving her consent. As a result of her humble obedience, Mary agrees to God's request to become the Mother of the Messiah. In her lowliness, she refers to herself as the handmaiden of the Lord. Not fully understanding the depths of God's plans for her, she still proceeds with faith in God by saying yes to His request, trusting totally in the providence and will of her Creator.

We can learn through the meditation of this mystery and through Mary's example, how to say "fiat" and give our lives fully to Christ with a deep sense of trust and abandonment.

Mary Speaks

What love I had for my Son, when I knew I was to become His Mother! Never had I dreamed that I would become the Mother of God, but so I was. How often I meditated on this marvelous act of the Creator's love for humanity. You, too, should reflect on this great mystery, which shows the awesome power of God. He loves you without reserve, so you must give of yourself to Him more abundantly. Ask Him to show you how to say yes in all things, no matter how great or small.

One Our Father, 10 Hail Mary's, Glory Be

2nd *Joyful Mystery - The Visitation*

Mary set out at once to visit her cousin, Elizabeth, upon the angel's message that her cousin had conceived in her old age. Mary believed in the angel's words without asking for proof. Why did Mary hasten to visit Elizabeth upon such hearing good news? We can imagine that Mary, being perfectly sensitive to the needs of other's, especially her cousin, and knowing that Elizabeth had grieved for so many years because of her barrenness, would now wish to congratulate her and rejoice with her at such a miracle.

Therefore, since the angel reveals this testimony of Elizabeth's pregnancy to Mary, she must have trusted it was God's will that she visit her cousin. Perhaps Mary desired also to share her secret with someone who had received a visitation from the same angel and who had also experienced a miraculous conception. And lastly, Mary, full of grace and charity, wished to minister to her cousin out of love and concern.

Scripture tells us that at the sound of Mary's greeting, the baby leapt in Elizabeth's womb. We know that Elizabeth used the same words when greeting Mary as the archangel, Gabriel did, "Blessed are you among women." The Church teaches us that John the Baptist was sanctified in the womb, at the moment Mary's greeting sounded in Elizabeth's ears.

Mother Teresa once said that God used this example of an unborn baby in scripture to announce Jesus' coming, in order to show the importance of life in the womb. Mary's illustration of visiting her cousin teaches us not to procrastinate in performing good works. Her humility upon hearing Elizabeth's salutation caused Mary to proclaim and to magnify God's mighty power working through her.

Should we not strive to be filled with the Holy Spirit, so we can imitate Elizabeth's greeting to Mary each time we receive Holy Communion, therefore saying: "How is it that my Lord and Savior should come to me?"

Before each daily reception of the Eucharist, I ask Our Lady to prepare my heart and hands to resemble hers so that I may welcome Jesus.

During the Advent Season, I ask her to make my hands like a cradle to receive him gently. During the Lenten Season, I ask her to help my hands receive Jesus, as she received him when he was taken down from the cross. And during the remainder of the Liturgical Season, I ask Our Lady to help make my hands become a throne to receive Jesus as my Lord and King.

How do you prepare to receive Jesus each time you go to Holy Communion?

Mary Speaks

What wondrous things God had done for my cousin, Elizabeth! Never had I reflected on His great miracles working through humanity, as I did when I was told that I would become the Savior's mother. Thus, my joy was united to my cousin's, when I was told also that Elizabeth had now conceived in her old age. Yes, my child, you too must reflect often on the wonders of your Savior. As God and King, He comes to you often. How little you receive Him with open hearts.

Open up your love for your neighbor and visit those who are sick or ailing. Jesus will come to them in the same way that He used me to visit my cousin.

My child, pray for the will to do more of God's work while here on earth.

One Our Father, 10 Hail Mary's, Glory Be

3rd *Joyful Mystery – The Birth of Jesus*

At the time of the census by the emperor Augustus, Mary and Joseph's name had to be inscribed at Bethlehem, since they were descended from the line of David. The distance from Nazareth to Jerusalem was approximately 70 miles. Imagine traveling that route by donkey or foot, on top of being pregnant with child! Have you ever had the slightest discomfort when traveling? Think of how Mary must have felt, being pregnant and with no modern convenience of travel.

The sufferings of Jesus began with His birth into the world. He was born in a stable with the severest poverty. For the Son of God to become human was an infinite humiliation, even if He had been born inside a royal palace and laid in a crib on the finest cushions of gold! However, Christ wished to humble himself even more, and therefore was born in a poor stable full of animals and laid in the rudest of cribs. The Lord and Master of the Universe, whose kingdom would have no end, was unable to find a place in the city of Bethlehem in which to be born!

Our Lord chose for himself this extreme poverty to make up for the sins of our pride, concupiscence of the eyes and flesh, and to give us an example of humility, self-denial, and mortification. Christ also wished to show us that the world is spiritually poor and that it needed enlightenment from its Creator. That is why in Luke 2:14, the angels sang, "Glory to God in the highest and on earth peace to those on whom his favor rests."

In the same way that the shepherds obeyed the angel and hastened to the stable, we too should obey the inward admonitions of grace and do what is right when we are prompted by God. Every day, I ask the Lord to make me sensitive to the promptings of the Holy Spirit and to guide me when making difficult decisions.

Mary Speaks

When I was about to give birth, my Savior was foremost in my mind. I wondered how I would hold Him and tell Him how much I loved Him. Joseph was beside me through it all, as my Savior did not wish for me to be alone.

Remember how much God wishes to use you to bring His love to others. St. Joseph will be beside you also, if you wish to give birth to Jesus in your hearts. It is only by saying yes to the will of the Father, that you can bear witness of Him to others.

Call upon the Christ Child more, when you need to remember how painful it is to be humiliated. Christ's infinite humiliation was not that He was born in a manger, but that He would be forgotten by many!

My children, do not forget the Christ Child, who has redeemed you and given birth to your hearts, so that you may live in utmost poverty while on earth, in order that you may enjoy the extreme riches of eternal glory.

One Our Father, 10 Hail Mary's, Glory Be

4th Joyful Mystery - The Visit of the Magi

During this mystery, let us meditate on the visit of the Wise Men. The Wise men, who followed the promptings of the star, offered gifts of gold, frankincense, and myrrh to the Christ child. In Israel, incense could only be burned before God alone!

The Magi offered gold to acknowledge God as a true king, and myrrh to testify their veneration of the human nature of Jesus. What do we give God to testify to our love for Him? Wouldn't God rather have our lives as sacrifices than any form of offering?

The Wise men, who cooperated with grace, found peace and fulfilment in their journey of searching for the Christ child. It is possible to believe, however, that there were others, who also saw the star, but were not moved enough to obey the divine invitation to seek out the Messiah as the Wise Men did. We should then ask ourselves; how often do we go in search of Jesus? How often do we obey the promptings of the Holy Spirit when we are given divine grace? Do we follow the star, the light that Christ has given us to worship Him and His Father?

If the Wise Men had not followed the star, which led them to Jesus, they would have remained in the dark. It was their obedience that caused them to seek out the Christ Child, and it was divine grace that allowed them to recognize Him in this tiny infant.

Therefore, let us keep our hearts open to the Sacraments, where the divine graces flow. Let us continually pray for the born and the unborn, that God will protect them from all modern day, King Herods, who seek to destroy the innocent, for their own selfish gain. How often do we imitate Mary and Joseph and the Wise Men and follow the law? Although Mary was sinless, she was obedient to the Jewish law. She did not wish to set herself apart, although she was the Mother of God!

How often do we feel superior to others because of our rank or standing, when we really are such lowly creatures in God's eyes? St. Francis of Assisi had a saying, which was, "We are who we are in God's eyes and no more." We should keep this in mind when the spirit of vanity and pride want to rule us! How much more of a recourse to Mary should we have when tempted to think we are above the law.

When we pray this mystery of the visit of the Magi, let us reflect on the love of our Savior and the infinite riches of His mercy, and what little we give Jesus in return.

Mary Speaks

My children, do not forget the Wise Men, who came bearing witness to the truth. You, too, are called to be children of your heavenly Father and bear witness to others. God does not ask of you extreme riches of gold, frankincense, and myrrh; only that of extreme poverty of heart.

Take heart to His example of teaching others the truth. The Wise Men's first inclination was to find the Christ Child upon hearing of His birth. Your first and foremost desire should be to spread this truth to others. As you come before your Savior, remember that the greatest gift you can offer of yourselves is your extreme poverty of heart and total abandonment to His will.

One Our Father, 10 Hail Mary's, Glory Be

5th Joyful Mystery - The Finding of the Child Jesus in the Temple

Each year, Jewish law required that every male Israelite, 12 years old and older, should go to Jerusalem for three principal feasts, which were mentioned in the Old Testament. Women were not required to go, but holy and pious women often liked to participate in the pilgrimage. Mary did not miss a chance to go to the sanctuary of the Lord, even though the journey was long and tiring. Thousands of pilgrims pressed through the gate at one time, making it very easy to lose sight of a family member.

Imagine what anxiety must have filled Mary and Joseph's hearts after discovering the loss of their son. Yet, think to what astonishment they later found Jesus, sitting alongside the doctors of the law, rather than in the crowd, answering questions with utmost authority and wisdom at such a young age. The Bible tells us:

When his parents saw him, they were astonished, and his mother said to him, "Son, why have you done this to us? Your father and I have been looking for you with great anxiety." And he said to them, "Why were you looking for me?

Did you not know that I must be in my
Father's house?"(Luke 2:48-49)

Like any loving parents, Joseph and Mary were
distraught after having lost their son. Have you
ever lost a child temporarily? When children
are little, they are often fearless. I have had the
frightening experience of losing sight of my
children when they were younger, even when I
tried to watch them closely. Mary and Joseph
know how that feels. Pray to them to help you
when your child has lost his or her way
spiritually. They know best how to search for
them and give you guidance and wisdom to
show your children where and how to look for
Jesus as they did.

The scriptures tell us that Jesus left and went
home with his parents and was obedient to
them. Imagine this thought; God is obedient to
man, rather than man obedient to God! Was
God trying to set an example for us? It seems
He was trying to give an appropriate
illustration for all children, no matter how
young or old. Although Mary and Joseph
searched for Jesus with much sorrow, it was
with much joy that they found Him! Let us
always search for Jesus, as Mary and Joseph
did, so we too can experience their joy. Where
and in what ways do you search for Jesus?

Mary Speaks

When I found my child in the temple, what joy flooded my soul! Jesus was never far from me after that. Can you imagine losing your loved one? My loss was nothing compared to the memorable experience of watching Him die on Calvary. What a great sense of loss and suffering filled my soul! That is what true suffering is; giving up your loved one when you know that no one even watches or cares.

Do you watch and care for my Son? He gave His all to you, so that you might be exposed to His love for all eternity. How little the world cares for my Son's love for them! You must watch and wait patiently with Me, as I watch and wait patiently with my Son for your return to Him. Know that you can give Him no greater pleasure than to seek Him out and find Him, and upon doing so, return His love with the fullest of measure.

Wait, my children, with my Son, and let Him know you love Him and care for Him, as I did.

One Our Father, 10 Hail Mary's, Glory Be

6th Joy - The Resurrection of Our Lord

After Jesus' death, His body was taken down from the cross and laid in the tomb for three days. On the third day, God the Father raised Jesus from the dead, by the power of the Holy Spirit.

Imagine Mary's great joy upon seeing her risen Son! The long awaited salvation for man was now made manifest for all eternity. Jesus had freed His people from sin and death.

Have you ever lost someone close to you, a relative or family member? I lost my husband to cancer, and I have lost several close friends of mine, whom I considered my spiritual fathers as well. I cried many tears at their death and funeral, but I have the consolation of knowing that I can still pray to them, and that they pray for me. I know that one day my sorrow will be turned into joy when we are reunited in heaven.

During this mystery, meditate on the joyous reunion that must have taken place between Mary and Jesus. Tears of happiness and love must have been exchanged so freely between them. Jesus' suffering was ended and was now turned into redemption for all of humanity. Have you ever pondered the great joy that you give Jesus when you recognize Him as your Savior? Each time you repent of your sins, all the angels and saints in heaven delight abundantly. Let us give thanks and praise for all the wonderful blessings God has given us through His suffering, death, and resurrection. It is a cause for rejoicing indeed!

Mary Speaks

It was upon great joy, that I recognized my Son, Jesus, risen from the dead. What great joy, indeed, filled my soul! My longing to be reunited with my Son in His physical body was at last attained. How I longed to hold Him so tight to Me.

My children, do you not wish to hold Jesus tight to your arms as well? Then show Him that you care about Him. Jesus has risen from the dead, my children! Why do you delay in greeting Him in the Eucharist of His love? His love is enormous for you! He wants to hold you tight and embrace you in His heart.

My children, return home to Jesus this very day. Make His heart glad indeed. As I greeted my Son upon His return from the grave, so too your life must be one of resurrection from the grave - the grave of sin and deceit, wickedness and destruction. Ask God to grant you everlasting life through this mystery of His rising from the dead.

One Our Father, 10 Hail Mary's, Glory Be

7th Joy – The Assumption and Coronation of the Blessed Virgin Mary

During this mystery, concentrate on the great longing of Christ and His Mother to be united again for all eternity. Mary was assumed body and soul into heaven after her earthly life was completed, because she was the perfect tabernacle for Jesus.

In the same way that the Ark of the Covenant in the Old Testament carried God's words, the Ten Commandments, so Mary carried the Ark of the New Covenant, Jesus. She was the perfect tabernacle of God's grace, and she now distributes those graces to all of us. Mary carried no stain of sin whatsoever throughout her life. How beautiful of a dwelling place she was for Jesus!

Mary is the Spouse of the Holy Spirit and the Mother of Our Lord and Savior. What wonderful and marvelous favors must accompany her magnificent power as the Mother of God! She is the spotless daughter of the Heavenly Father and the mediator of the Son for us. She dwells now in heaven as the dispenser of all graces.

St. Augustine says that Christ, when deigning to establish virginity in the heart of the Church, first preserved virginity in the body of Mary. How blessed we are to have a Mother who intercedes for us at the right hand of our Creator.

As we meditate on the joys of Mary and her love for us, let us remember that the soul, who is more intimately united to Mary, is also more closely united to the Lord, our God!

Mary Speaks

As I was crowned Queen of heaven and earth, I thought of all the ways my Son had exalted Me! Although His lowly handmaid, I was to become the Queen of all humanity.

The thought of many miracles flooded my soul at the reflection of my Son's kindness upon man, and how He elevated my soul to represent His.

This is beyond human imaginings, to be given the dignity of representing all humanity as their Queen and Mother. How grateful I am to God for giving me this privilege of being His handmaiden.

How grateful are you, my children, now that you have been raised to the dignity of Christ's love for you? Do you often quarrel about silly things, not acting in a manner fitting of your Lord and Savior? He has ransomed you at a great price. Show Him how much you return His love by acting in the dignity you were called to uphold.

As you meditate on this mystery, remember how great God's love is for you and for all of humanity.

One Our Father, 10 Hail Mary's, Glory Be

The Value of the Rosary

Each time, we recite the Hail Mary we give Our Lady exceedingly great joy. And she, in turn, listens to our prayers and answers us. How truly blessed we are to have such a loving and caring spiritual Mother.

Each time I pray the rosary, I can reflect on Mary's holiness, and I ask my guardian angel and all the saints to pray with me. The thirteenth promise of the rosary is that we will have the whole celestial court praying with us when we pray the rosary, and also they will pray for us at the hour of our death. What a great consolation to know we have such powerful intercessors in heaven.

On the following page, you will find the fifteen promises of Our Lady to those who pray the rosary, but more importantly, to those who pray with the heart.

THE FIFTEEN PROMISES
OF THE ROSARY
(GIVEN TO ST. DOMINIC AND BLESSED ALAN)

1. To all those who shall pray my Rosary devoutly, I promise my special protection and great graces.

2. Those who shall persevere in the recitation of my Rosary will receive some special grace.

3. The Rosary will be a very powerful armor against hell; it will destroy vice, deliver from sin and dispel heresy.

4. The rosary will make virtue and good works flourish, and will obtain for souls the most abundant divine mercies. It will draw the hearts of men from the love of the world and its vanities, and will lift them to the desire of eternal things. Oh, that souls would sanctify themselves by this means.

5. Those who trust themselves to me through the Rosary will not perish.

6. Whoever recites my Rosary devoutly reflecting on the mysteries, shall never be overwhelmed by misfortune. He will not experience the anger of God nor will he perish by an unprovided death. The sinner will be converted; the just will persevere in grace and merit eternal life.

7. Those truly devoted to my Rosary shall not die without the sacraments of the Church.

8. Those who are faithful to recite my Rosary shall have during their life and at their death the light of God and the plenitude of His graces and will share in the merits of the blessed.

9. I will deliver promptly from purgatory souls devoted to my Rosary.

10. True children of my Rosary will enjoy great glory in heaven.

11. What you shall ask through my Rosary you shall obtain.

12. To those who propagate my Rosary I promise aid in all their necessities.

13. I have obtained from my Son that all the members of the Rosary Confraternity shall have as their intercessors, in life and in death, the entire celestial court.

14. Those who recite my Rosary faithfully are my beloved children, the brothers and sisters of Jesus Christ.

15. Devotion to my Rosary is a special sign of predestination.

Regarding the Holy Rosary, Sister Lucia, said in an interview on December 26, 1957 to Fr. Fuentes: "Look Father, the Most Holy Virgin in these last times in which we live has given new efficacy in the meditation of the Holy Rosary. She has given this efficacy to such an extent that there is no problem, no matter how difficult it is, whether temporal or above all spiritual, in the personal life of each one of us, of our families, of the families of the work, or of the religious communities, or even of the life of the people and nations that cannot be solved by the rosary. There is no problem, I tell you, no matter how difficult it is, that we cannot solve by the prayer of the Holy Rosary. With the Holy Rosary, we will save ourselves. We will sanctify ourselves. We will console Our Lord and obtain the salvation of many souls."

What a powerful reflection on the holy rosary of Our Lady. While meditating on the scripture passages with the rosary, invite Mary to come dwell in your soul and make you one with Jesus. She will do so willingly and with great love in her heart for you and her crucified Lord.

Remember the requests she has given you in each meditation. As your Mother, she knows best what your soul needs to resemble Him who created you and redeemed you. Never hesitate to fly to Mary's patronage, as she is the rescuer of lost souls and Mother to all.

Mary, Our Queen, *Our Mother*, pray for us!

St. Joseph, Patron of the *Universal Church*, protect us!

Printed in Great Britain
by Amazon